Life in the Time of

Franklin D. Roosevelt
and the
Great Depression

Heinemann Library
Chicago, Illinois

© 2008 Heinemann Library
a division of Reed Elsevier Inc.
Chicago, Illinois

Customer Service 888-454-2279

Visit our website at www.heinemannlibrary.com

Designed by Kimberly R. Miracle and Betsy Wernert.
Printed in China by South China Printing.

11 10 09 08
10 9 8 7 6 5 4 3 2

Library of Congress Cataloging-in-Publication Data
DeGezelle, Terri, 1955-
   Franklin D. Roosevelt and the Great Depression / Terri DeGezelle.
      p. cm. -- (Life in the time of)
   Includes bibliographical references and index.
   ISBN 978-1-4034-9670-6 (hc) -- ISBN 978-1-4034-9678-2 (pb)
   1. Roosevelt, Franklin D. (Franklin Delano), 1882-1945--Juvenile
literature. 2. Presidents--United States--Biography--Juvenile literature.
3. Depressions--1929--United States--Juvenile literature. 4. United
States--Economic conditions--1918-1945--Juvenile literature. 5. New Deal,
1932-1939--Juvenile literature. I. Title.
   E806.D428 2007
   973.917092--dc22
   [B]
                              2006102472

Acknowledgments
The author and publishers are grateful to the following for permission to reproduce copyright material: **p. 4** Corbis, **p. 5** Corbis/Bettmann, **p. 6** Corbis, **p. 7** Corbis/Bettmann, **p. 8** Corbis/Bettmann, **p. 9** Corbis/Bettmann, **p. 10** Corbis/Bettmann, **p. 11** Corbis, **p. 13** Corbis, **p. 14** Corbis/Hulton-Deutsch Collection, **p. 15** Corbis/Bettmann, **p. 16** Corbis/Bettmann, **p. 17** Corbis/Lester Lefkowitz, **p. 18** Corbis/Hulton-Deutsch Colleciton, **p. 19** Corbis Sygma/Bettmann, **p. 20** Corbis/Bettmann, **p. 21** Corbis/Bettmann, **p. 22** Corbis/Bettmann, **p. 23** Corbis, **p. 24** Library of Congress, **p. 25** Library of Congress/Chase-Statler, Washington, **p. 26** Corbis, **p. 27** Corbis/Bettmann.

Map illustration on page 12 by Mapping Specialists, Ltd.

Cover photograph of Franklin Delano Roosevelt reproduced with permission of the Library of Congress. Cover photograph of Salvation Army relief workers at a soup kitchen during the Great Depression reproduced with permission of Empics/AP.

The author dedicates this book to Richard Longenecker.

Every effort has been made to contact copyright holders of any material reproduced in this book. Any omissions will be rectified in subsequent printings if notice is given to the publisher.

Disclaimer
All Internet addresses (URLs) given in this book were valid at the time of going to press. However, due to the dynamic nature of the Internet, some addresses may have changed or ceased to exist since publication. While the author and the publishers regret any inconvenience this may cause readers, no responsibility for any such changes can be accepted by either the author or the publishers.

Contents

Some words are shown in bold, **like this**. You can find out what they mean by looking in the glossary.

Meet Franklin D. Roosevelt

Franklin Delano Roosevelt was born on January 30, 1882. He was an only child and grew up in Hyde Park, New York. Franklin D. Roosevelt married Eleanor Roosevelt and they had six children.

Franklin D. Roosevelt had an illness called **polio**, which made walking difficult.

In 1933 Roosevelt became the 32nd president of the United States. He was president for 12 years — longer than any other president. He became president during the **Great Depression**. This was a time when life was very hard for many people.

Franklin D. Roosevelt was president from 1933 to 1945.

A Growing Country

In the 1920s, the United States was a growing country. Many people had jobs and plenty of money. Stores sold new **inventions**. Farmers bought bigger and better farm machinery to farm more land.

In the 1920s, farmers grew enough food for everyone.

People had money
to buy cars.

Families began buying cars. Workers built new roads and highways. Some families took vacations for the first time in their lives. Everyone was excited about the future, but then it all stopped.

Black Tuesday

In the 1920s, many people put their money in the **stock market**. The stock market is a place where people buy and sell **shares**. Shares are parts of a company. On October 29, 1929, something happened to the stock market.

People who had put their money in the stock market now had big problems.

Many people wanted to sell all their shares, but no one wanted to buy any shares. This made the stock market **crash**. Many people lost all of their money. October 29, 1929 was called Black Tuesday because it was such a bad day for many people.

When the stock market crashed, banks ran out of money and closed.

The Great Depression

In 1929 the **Great Depression** started when the **stock market crashed**. Many people lost their jobs. Families did not have money to pay their bills or buy food. Farmers did not have money to buy farm machinery.

Many people waited in long lines to get free food.

Some children could not go to school. They worked to help their families get money. Some families went without shoes and warm clothes for the winter. People had no money for doctor visits or other important things.

Children had few toys or games to play with during the Great Depression.

Dust Covers the Land

This map shows the area known as the Dust Bowl.

In the 1930s, there was no rain for a long time. The soil dried up and turned to dust. Winds blew the dust across the **Great Plains**. People called the Great Plains the **Dust Bowl** because of all the dust.

Dust covered everything in its path, even houses.

Without rain, farmers could not grow **crops**. Without crops to sell, farmers could not buy food and clothes. Without shoppers, store owners closed their stores. Many people had to pack up and move.

The New Deal

In 1933 Franklin D. Roosevelt became president of the United States. He wanted to help the people of the United States. He knew people needed homes and jobs. In his first 100 days of being president, Roosevelt put his New Deal **programs** into action.

Franklin D. Roosevelt had a plan to help the people of the United States.

Franklin D. Roosevelt was the first president to use the radio to talk to Americans.

The New Deal was a group of programs to help the United States. President Roosevelt used the radio to tell the American people about his ideas. People had hope after they listened to Roosevelt explain his New Deal programs.

Jobs for Many

The New Deal programs put many people to work.

During the **Great Depression**, many people lost their jobs. The New Deal helped people find new jobs. Workers were paid for the work that they did. With their pay, workers could buy food and clothes.

The Hoover Dam was one of the New Deal projects.

Many people went to work with the New Deal's **programs**. Some workers built new roads, hospitals, and state parks. Other workers planted seeds on farmlands to help farmers grow food.

Attack on Pearl Harbor

In 1939 most of the world was fighting in a war called World War Two. More than 70 countries were fighting. The United States was not at war. The United States had soldiers and ships at Pearl Harbor, Hawaii.

Many soldiers were fighting in a huge war far away from the United States.

Many ships and airplanes were destroyed
in the attack on Pearl Harbor.

Early on December 7, 1941, the country of Japan
bombed Pearl Harbor. People heard Japanese
airplanes above them. Pearl Harbor was under
attack. Many American soldiers died in the attack.

The United States Goes to War

President Roosevelt learned Pearl Harbor was **bombed**. He started to make plans for war. He gave a speech to the American people to explain that the United States was going to war. On December 8, 1941, the United States **declared** war on Japan.

President Roosevelt wore a black armband to show he was sad about the American soldiers who died in Pearl Harbor.

After Roosevelt's speech, many men left their jobs to join the **military**. Men waited in long lines to join the military. The country needed to get ready for war. Soldiers needed airplanes, ships, and tanks to fight the war.

Many people signed up to fight in the war.

Everyone Works Together

No job was too hard for women workers during the war.

Before the war, most women stayed home to take care of children. When men went to be soldiers, women took over their jobs outside of the home. **Equipment** needed to be built for the soldiers. Women built airplanes, ships, and guns.

People waited in long lines to get their rationing coupons.

In 1942 Franklin D. Roosevelt told Americans that gasoline, sugar, and rubber tires had to be **rationed**. Rationing gave a little bit to everyone. Everyone got the same amount. Rationing made sure the soldiers had what they needed to fight the war.

President Roosevelt Dies

On April 12, 1945, Franklin D. Roosevelt was on vacation in Warm Springs, Georgia. An artist was painting Roosevelt's picture when he said he didn't feel well. He died later that afternoon.

Thousands of Americans gathered to honor Franklin D. Roosevelt.

Harry S. Truman was president from 1945 to 1953.

Americans had lost a good friend. Vice President Harry S. Truman became the 33rd president of the United States. President Truman was the new leader of a country at war. He had to make many hard decisions.

The War Ends

On August 14, 1945, countries agreed to stop fighting the war. Many people had died. Now that World War Two was over, there was peace in the world. Soldiers came home to their families.

President Truman told newspaper reporters that the war was over.

The **Great Depression** ended when the war began. People got new jobs making supplies for the war. People had money to buy food and pay their bills. The Great Depression was over.

Americans celebrated the end of World War Two.

If You Grew Up Long Ago

If you grew up in the time of Franklin D. Roosevelt…

- You may have only known one president while growing up. Franklin D. Roosevelt was president for 12 years.

- You would have learned that there were only 48 states. Alaska and Hawaii didn't become states until 1959.

- Your mother may have sewn your clothes on a sewing machine.

- You and your family would have sat down to listen to the radio after dinner.

- You may have received a Slinky as a gift. Richard James invented the Slinky in 1943.

Timeline

1882   Franklin D. Roosevelt is born.

1929   The **stock market crashes**. The **Great Depression** begins.

1930s The **Dust Bowl** begins in the **Great Plains**.

1933   Franklin D. Roosevelt becomes the 32nd president. The New Deal is explained to the American people.

1939   World War Two begins.

1941   December 7: Pearl Harbor, Hawaii is **bombed**.

December 8: The United States goes to war.

1942   President Roosevelt tells Americans to **ration** gasoline, sugar, and tires.

1945   April 12: Franklin D. Roosevelt dies.

April 12: Harry S. Truman becomes the 33rd president.

August 14: World War Two ends.

Find Out More

Books

Ford, Carin T. *Franklin D. Roosevelt: The 32nd President*. Berkeley Heights: NJ, 2006.

Isaacs, Sally Senzell. *Life in the Dust Bowl*. Chicago: Heinemann Library, 2002.

Mara, Wil. *Franklin D. Roosevelt*. New York: Children's Press, 2004.

Schaefer, Ted and Lola Schaefer. *The Franklin Delano Roosevelt Memorial*. Chicago: Heinemann Library, 2006.

Websites

Franklin D. Roosevelt Presidential Library and Museum
http://www.fdrlibrary.marist.edu/educat33.html

Library of Congress – Depression and WWII
http://www.americaslibrary.gov/cgi-bin/page.cgi/jb/wwii

White House Kids – Meet the Presidents
http://www.whitehouse.gov/kids/presidents/franklindroosevelt.html

Glossary

attack try to hurt someone by fighting

bomb blow something up

crash when something breaks or fails

crop plant grown by farmers for food and other uses

declare announce something

Dust Bowl time when there was little rain. The dirt of the Great Plains area turned to dust and farmers could not grow any crops.

equipment tools and machinery, such as those needed by soldiers

Great Depression (1929–1939) hard time in the history of the United States when many people did not have jobs or money

Great Plains area of land in the middle of the United States

invention something new and useful that did not exist before

military group of soldiers and equipment. In the United States, the military includes the Army, Navy, Air Force, Marine Corps, and Coast Guard.

polio disease that makes a person's muscles weak. Today there is medicine to stop polio.

program plan for doing something

ration give the same amount of something to everyone

share part of a company that you can buy

stock market place where people buy and sell shares

Index